# 31 Days to an Organized *Life*

Brenda Prinzavalli

Organizing Strategist

Copyright © 2013 Brenda Prinzavalli

All rights reserved.

ISBN-13: 978-0989123907
ISBN-10: 0989123901

## DEDICATION

Joyfully dedicated to my
spectacular husband, Brian,
my loving family, incredible friends
and the wonderful people I get to meet while
sharing organization with the world!
-Brenda Prinzavalli

# CONTENTS

| | |
|---|---|
| Purpose & Getting Started | vi |
| De-Clutter | 9 |
| Digital | 21 |
| Financial | 31 |
| Home | 39 |
| Personal | 55 |
| Schedule/Time | 67 |
| Checklist | 86 |
| Organizing Resources | 87 |

## Purpose

Everyone feels the same pain of dedicating time to get organized since it seems harder than finding a needle in a haystack! We wait for that one big opportunity to just tackle it all. Well, I need to break it to you; there's good news and not so good news.

The **not so good** news is that the next time you actually have that big block of time is likely not until next year…or the year after that…..if you're lucky.

The **good news** is that you don't have to wait for that one big block of time to get organized! That's right! You can actually get started THIS MONTH and take action to Reclaim Your Sanity! You can do it by taking focused actions in a short span of time.

## Getting Started

I am excited you want to get started and I can provide support for you in creating more organization in your busy life. Here are suggestions on how to use these actions for this powerful month of getting organized!

**Organizing Action Categories:**

De-Clutter
Digital
Financial
Home
Personal
Schedule/Time

There are 30 organizing actions divided into 6 main categories. One action is scheduled to cover 2 days; therefore you have a total of 31 days of actions toward having a more organized life!

**15+ minutes or 60+ minutes**

The amount of time it will take each one of you to complete these mini organizing projects will be different. To give you a quick reference to the estimated amount of time, each project has either a stopwatch or a calendar day icon. As you flip through the different projects, it will help you zero in on your project for the day.

 Tasks estimated to take 15–60 minutes

 Tasks estimated to take more than 60 minutes

**Order of completion**

There is no correct order of completion for these organizing projects. First, select the Organizing Action Category that you feel like taking on for the day. Then look at the time options for each task and select either a stopwatch (15+ min) or a calendar day (60+ min) based on the amount of time you have available and which one sounds most interesting for you that day.

**Your Results**

As you take on these mini-organizing projects you will have a wonderful sense of accomplishment and I want you to celebrate completing each task. In the days that follow organizing one aspect of your life, you will feel the benefits and positive results they create in your life. You will start to find your daily life becomes less stressful and you have more time!

**Let's get started!**

Other little de-clutter actions

*Put away or hang up clothes on your floor*

*Hold family members responsible for their own belongings. If each person picks up their belongings clutter won't start*

Group Done ☐

# De-Clutter

- Find 10

- Organize Your Car

- Saving Trees, One Catalog at a Time

- Tiny Slips of Paper

- Return Time

# Find 10

You might have heard of a de-clutter strategy that is related to a project that focuses on the connection between de-cluttering and abundance. It suggests that you give away one thing every day. At first it may sound like a lot, but think of all the things you bring into your environment, you probably bring in more than one item a day.

What if you were limited to bringing in one new thing a day? Well, first, you might be at the store a whole lot more, but my guess is you might actually bring fewer things into your environment.

One of the biggest culprits for clutter and disorganization is too much stuff! The critical thing to remember about having stuff is that you have to move the **stuff**, clean around the **stuff**, put the **stuff** back where it belongs, etc. Today, you take control of the **stuff** and reduce its negative impact on your space!

Take 20 minutes and find at least 10 things to return, donate, recycle or throw away or any other applicable exit strategy for extra stuff!

Look for items that:

- you haven't used in a long time
- don't fit anymore
- you don't like
- won't use
- have something new and better
- are part of something that you will not complete
- are related to an old hobby or activity

# NOTES                                Done ☐

_____

_____

_____

_____

## Tasks to Complete

☐ _____

☐ _____

☐ _____

☐ _____

## Other Projects Sparked by this Task

_____

_____

_____

Today I am celebrating my accomplishment by:

_____

# Organize Your Car

It is time for you to head out to organize a place where some of us spend way too much time. This organizing task is to clean out one or more storage areas in your car.

Your organizing task for today depends on:

- Your car
- Your past "violations" of the messy sort and
- How much time you have.


You can clean out one compartment that you use the most or you can be brave and venture into the compartment that you haven't opened in quite some time. If you have a little extra time you might just organize the trunk as well!

31 Days to an Organized Life

# NOTES     Done ☐

_____

_____

_____

_____

## Tasks to Complete

☐ _____

☐ _____

☐ _____

☐ _____

## Other Projects Sparked by this Task

_____

_____

_____

Today I am celebrating my accomplishment by:

_____

# Saving Trees, One Catalog at a Time

If you are like most people, you receive your fair share of trees in the form of catalogs. Did you think you were collecting a small forest? To add insult to injury, you might have more than one catalog from an individual company. Catalog shopping does save you time and gas, but what does it cost in trees?

What is an organized person to do?

1) Recycle catalogs that:
- you have completely finished using
- are out of date
- you have multiple copies

2) Get off mailing lists
- contact catalog companies to request removing from their mailing list
- visit the company website and follow instructions for Mailing List Removal

3) Digital Catalogs
- Create your own "catalog rack" by bookmarking favorite company websites
- Create an email folder for emails related to your favorite shopping online

## NOTES

Done ☐

_____

_____

_____

_____

### Tasks to Complete

☐ _____

☐ _____

☐ _____

☐ _____

### Other Projects Sparked by this Task

_____

_____

_____

Today I am celebrating my accomplishment by:

_____

Brenda Prinzavalli

# Tiny Slips of Paper

Find a different solution for all those tiny slips of paper.

Yes, we all have them and some have them more than others. It's the phone number, the reminder on the little phone memo sheet to pick up TP on the way home, the short To Do list of the "really" important tasks for the day and the notes you took about flight times for your next trip.

Here's the problem with tiny slips of paper:

- one of them can get easily lost
- you have to look through the whole stack again and again to find the one you need
- they are different sizes, shapes, colors and various stages of "stickiness" if it was a sticky note
- most important - they don't give you a message of being organized!

For tips and ideas, visit the website for more suggestions on managing quick notes on our Resources page.

www.balorg.com

31 Days to an Organized Life

# NOTES    Done ☐

_____

_____

_____

_____

## Tasks to Complete

☐ _____

☐ _____

☐ _____

☐ _____

## Other Projects Sparked by this Task

_____

_____

_____

Today I am celebrating my accomplishment by:

_____

Brenda Prinzavalli

# Return Time!

Look around your home or office and collect items that belong to someone else! You will find overdue books, videos, and items you borrowed from someone else whether a colleague, family, friend or neighbor.

- Make a list of the items to return and to whom they belong.

- Then put a basket/tote in your trunk to hold the items to return that are on your list so you have them with you as you go about your busy day. If you just put them in the basket in the trunk without making the list, they might end up forgotten and still in your space!

## NOTES    Done ☐

_____

_____

_____

_____

### Tasks to Complete

☐ _____

☐ _____

☐ _____

☐ _____

### Other Projects Sparked by this Task

_____

_____

_____

Today I am celebrating my accomplishment by:

_____

## Other little digital actions

*Backup digital files*

*Explore what areas of your life can be streamlined with automation*

Group Done ☐

# Digital

- Organize Computer Area

- Update Contact Information

- Organize Digital Files

- Electronic Challenge No More

# Organize Computer Area

Take 15 minutes and empower your computer time by organizing your computer space!

For Desktop users
- Take off all the sticky notes around the screen and put that info where it belongs.
- If you have a raised platform for your monitor, I bet there's something under it, in it, or on top of it. Time to sort and tidy that up.
- If you have something inspirational in your computer space, do a quick check to make sure it's still empowering you as you first intended. If you really don't look at it anymore, maybe it needs to inspire you somewhere else.
- When it's cleared of papers, sticky notes, misc office supplies, etc, take a minute to dust it off, clean the screen with a screen safe wipe, clean the surface underneath and make sure the hard drive unit is dust free as well.

For the non-Desktop users.
- Clean up your laptop case: check pockets, wrap cables with Velcro bungees, clear out, etc.
- Verify you have identification on your mobile unit. If not, get ID on it ASAP!
- Verify you have the serial number of your mobile unit in some other location than on your unit or electronically saved there.
- If you use your laptop while sitting on a couch, in a chair or at the kitchen counter, do a quick clean up of that space as it will likely accumulate extra cables, papers, coffee cups, etc.

31 Days to an Organized Life

# NOTES    Done ☐

_____

_____

_____

## Tasks to Complete

☐ _____

☐ _____

☐ _____

☐ _____

## Other Projects Sparked by this Task

_____

_____

_____

Today I am celebrating my accomplishment by:

_____

# Update Contact Information

Contacts, Phone Numbers, Emails, IM names, Twitter Name, etc! They are everywhere, yet are they the same in all your contact storage locations?

Take 15 minutes to update as many entries of contact information in your phone, email contacts, address book or any other database. There might even be a letter or greeting card you've received and noticed a new return address so you tore off the corner to update in your contacts!

The second step is to check in with your sync process between devices. Is it working properly?

It's an ongoing process to keep your contacts up to date and starting with 15 minutes today, then maybe 15 minutes each day for the rest of the week or even month can get you on the right track for keeping your contact information organized and synced for the rest of the year!

31 Days to an Organized Life

# NOTES                                    Done ☐

_____

_____

_____

_____

## Tasks to Complete

☐ _____

☐ _____

☐ _____

☐ _____

## Other Projects Sparked by this Task

_____

_____

_____

Today I am celebrating my accomplishment by:

_____

# Organize Digital Files

Have you recently searched for a digital document .....

    for too long?

Do you have folders and ways to separate your digital files?

Do you have duplicates of digital documents or files?

In this ever increasing digital age, we are just as likely to have a "stack of papers" hiding in digital format. You've seen it, the unending list of files that you have to scan over and over to find the one you're looking for. The bonus is that you can search by key word, sort them by alphabetical or date, but it can still be a longer search than necessary. Take control of your digital files, it's just as important as managing your paper files.

- Make sure you have folders with consistent names
- Put files into folders
- Check for duplicate files
- Delete unnecessary files

GOOD NEWS! Studies show that it is 10-15% easier to retrieve a digital file than a paper file. Keeping your digital world organized can maintain or even increase that percentage! Easier is good!

The last comment about digital files is that you MUST back up your digital information! Set a schedule or pattern to back up your information if you don't have an automatic backup system in place

## NOTES     Done ☐

_____

_____

_____

_____

### Tasks to Complete

☐ _____

☐ _____

☐ _____

☐ _____

### Other Projects Sparked by this Task

_____

_____

_____

Today I am celebrating my accomplishment by:

_____

Brenda Prinzavalli

# Electronic Challenge No More

Do you love it? Do you hate it? Technology that is. Now hate is a pretty strong word, but I'm likely not alone in my occasional use of nasty words directed toward my technology or electronics. Yes, we love what technology can do for us and yet we all can have a moment when we get frustrated by it.

Years ago I made a pact with myself that I would never let technology get the best of me. It does brink on the edge of getting the best of me at times, but I learned there is always a solution.... you just have to find it!

Let's find a solution for you that doesn't involve electrocution, a trip to the store to buy a new computer or an entire bar of dark chocolate to ease your tension!

Questions to help you get started:

- If there is one glitch that has been bugging you about an electronic in your life, it's time to take care of it.
- If there is a process that a piece of software can do for you, but you don't know how, learn it.
- If you have a new piece of software or hardware that you have not installed, activated, plugged in or downloaded, do it!

Where can you find the answers?

- Manuals - paper
- Manuals - digital
- Technology Consultants & Trainers
- Online support from corporations
- Online support from question boards, chat rooms
- Ask a teenager!

## NOTES                                   Done ☐

_____

_____

_____

_____

### Tasks to Complete

☐ _____

☐ _____

☐ _____

☐ _____

### Other Projects Sparked by this Task

_____

_____

_____

Today I am celebrating my accomplishment by:

_____

## Other little financial actions

*Take receipts out of your wallet everyday*

*Use email or text alerts for financial accounts to bring activity to your attention.*

Group Done ☐

# Financial

- Create a Tax File

- Purse or Wallet Refresh

- Organize Your "Other" Money

# Create a Tax File

The season for tax preparation comes around faster than expected. Throughout the year you will have documents to collect related to filing your taxes whether business or personal.

Create a TAX file now so you can have a holding place for tax related documents such as:

- Charitable donation receipts
- Correspondence from the IRS
- Changes in your mortgage(s) or other loans
- Receipts or invoices considered tax deductable
- Investment income
- Jury duty
- Gambling winnings
- Scholarship information

As the year draws to a close and rolls into the New Year, you will receive year end statements and other documents needed to complete your taxes.

Suggestions for this folder:

- Make it a bright colored or at least a different colored folder
- The very front of a file drawer is a great place for it.
- Let anyone and everyone in your family know where it is located. Then whoever gets the mail, opens statements or has documents that need to be included in the TAXES CURRENT YEAR file can support the gathering of this critical information!

## NOTES

Done ☐

_____

_____

_____

_____

## Tasks to Complete

☐ _____

☐ _____

☐ _____

☐ _____

## Other Projects Sparked by this Task

_____

_____

_____

Today I am celebrating my accomplishment by:

_____

Brenda Prinzavalli

# Purse or Wallet Refresh

It's time to pay attention to one of the most important financial data centers in your life: your purse or wallet! There are a couple of tasks related to this project.

<u>Copy</u>
First and most important is to make a copy (front & back) of all Credit Cards, Driver's License and any other important cards you carry in your wallet. Lay them out on a copy machine and before you press COPY make sure the setting for color isn't too dark. Most cards have a lot of color on them and you want to be able to read the numbers. The trick is to help it copy into 2 dimensional readability instead of 3 dimensional. Don't forget to do the backside as well!

This now serves as your backup copy of the items you carry in your wallet. Put copies in a safe location in case your wallet is stolen or misplaced. This is also a great thing to do before you go on a trip!

<u>Clean</u>
Before you slip those cards back in your wallet and since you have most items out of your wallet anyway, go ahead and take everything else out. If this is your purse, yes take EVERYTHING out.

It is also important to clean the **outside** of your purse or wallet. Reports show germs and bacteria can linger on your personal financial datacenter! It's pretty disgusting!

As you replace the cards in your wallet, take a fresh look and see if things can be rearranged to make better use of the space or to make it easier for you to use. For example, put the Bank Card you use the most in the slot that you can access with the most ease. Then it is easy to slip it out and in every time you go to use it.

31 Days to an Organized Life

## NOTES
Done ☐

_____

_____

_____

_____

## Tasks to Complete

☐ _____

☐ _____

☐ _____

☐ _____

## Other Projects Sparked by this Task

_____

_____

_____

Today I am celebrating my accomplishment by:

_____

# Organize Your "Other" Money!
# Gift Certificates, Gift Cards, Credit Receipts, Coupons

You likely received at least one Gift Card for a gift, thank you or from returning a gift and receiving store credit. This is a good time to make sure you have an organized way to keep track of them.

This is your MONEY! Coupons or Discount Certificates can also fall into this category as they are money in your pocket if you shop or dine with a retailer offering a coupon! Find one safe and easy-to-remember location for these items.

The three main categories with this type of gift or money are to remember:

- that you have them,
- when they expire and
- where you have stashed them.

One idea is to simply put them in an envelope or a file folder labeled <u>Gift Certificates, Gift Cards, Credit Receipts.</u> If you have too many to look through on a regular basis, here are some possible ways to divide them.

- By the category; Food, Clothing, Personal Services, Office Stores, Misc
- By the type; Gift Cert, Gift Card, etc
- Alphabetical by store
- By expiration date. Not the top choice, but it might be the one that works for you.

31 Days to an Organized Life

# NOTES

Done ☐

_____

_____

_____

_____

## Tasks to Complete

☐ _____

☐ _____

☐ _____

☐ _____

## Other Projects Sparked by this Task

_____

_____

_____

Today I am celebrating my accomplishment by:

_____

Brenda Prinzavalli

## Other little home actions

*Throw out old pairs or single socks.*

*Put away or hang up clothes on your floor or tossed on a chair*

*Clean off the refrigerator.*

Group Done ☐

# Home

- Organize Your Workout Bag

- First Aid and Medical Supplies

- Organize the #&$%* Drawer

- Organize Your Nightstand

- Organize Your Bathroom Counter

Brenda Prinzavalli

# Organize Your Workout Bag

Fitness and Health are on most people's list of goals; let's do some organizing to support them! Reports state that if you have a packed and supplied workout bag it will dramatically increase your chance of working out!

If you don't have a workout bag because you work out at home, you still have a task today. It is time for you to clean out and organize your home work out area and equipment.

Empty and clean out:
- All pockets
- Cosmetic and toiletry bags
- Mini-pouch for money, ID/Membership cards
- If the bag is washable, wash it. If NOT, wipe out the inside.

Refresh basics:
- Refill or get new toiletry bottles
- Restock paper products such as Q-tips, cotton balls, feminine products, etc
- Put in a few pair of clean socks and under garments

**Most Common Gym Bag Contents**

For your workout session:
gym membership card
lock
workout clothes
exercise gloves,
hair ties, hat or headband
iPod/ MP3 player
training log
bottled water
small towel
gum

If you shower at the gym:
bath towel
shower shoes
soap
razor
deodorant
makeup &, lotion
comb and/or brush
blow dryer, curling iron
change of clothes
snack for post workout

**If you work out at home**, clean and organize your workout room or storage area for workout equipment and supplies.
Spend 15 minutes:
- create a new storage solution if supplies are not organized
- get rid of items that don't belong there
- bring back items that migrated out of the space
- sort reading materials

31 Days to an Organized Life

# NOTES           Done ☐

_____

_____

_____

_____

## Tasks to Complete

☐ _____

☐ _____

☐ _____

☐ _____

## Other Projects Sparked by this Task

_____

_____

_____

Today I am celebrating my accomplishment by:

_____

"I bring simple solutions into my home and life!"

# First Aid and Medical Supplies

This organizing project may take one or two days because there are several steps: assess what you need, purchase items and assemble kits.

> *One word of caution:*
> *Be careful of animals and small children!!*
> *Do not allow them to have access to these*
> *medical supplies as you work on this project.*

Having appropriate first aid supplies follows one of my organizing philosophies: Be Organized, Be Prepared! The organizing project is to bring all <u>First Aid Kits</u> and <u>Medical Supply Kits</u> up to date.

Your home, office, and car need a basic <u>First Aid Kit</u> and home also needs a <u>Medical Supply Kit</u>. From bumps and scrapes to scratchy throats and fevers, nothing says organized more than a household with well stocked kits!

It is a good idea to first determine the needs of your unique household. You may have pets, larger families, sports, work environments, outdoor activities or a family member with special needs.

1) Review <u>First Aid Kit</u> and <u>Medical Supply Kit</u> recommendations you can find on many emergency preparedness websites or you can visit our page specifically for this topic. Find it in the Resources tab and then select Organizing Strategies and Tips. It has links to various sites that provide appropriate guidelines and preferred lists for your specific needs.

2) Gather and review your current supplies. Find out what you already own so you don't buy duplicates.

3) Once you have a list printed and prepared, it's time to purchase needed items and assemble your kits.

## First Aid and Medical Supplies (cont.)

This organizing project is about being prepared for mishaps and basic medical emergencies. There are other emergency kits that everyone should consider assembling such as:

- Natural Disasters
- Pandemic
- Home Fires
- Technological & Accidental Hazards
- Terrorist Hazards

## NOTES

Done ☐

_____

_____

_____

_____

## Tasks to Complete

☐ _____

☐ _____

☐ _____

☐ _____

## Other Projects Sparked by this Task

_____

_____

_____

Today I am celebrating my accomplishment by:

_____

Brenda Prinzavalli

# Organize the Most Frustrating Drawer

This task is about "that" drawer. Yes, you all know exactly which one I'm talking about! It's that drawer that causes you the most frustration, the one that you spend the most amount of time at because it takes you so long to find something in it, and yes, cover your ears, the drawer that you swear at.

**Today is the day to take it on and make a change!**

Suggested questions to help create a different pattern:

Why have things collected here?

Do they actually belong someplace else and this was just an easy place to dump something?

Do you need to separate the items in the drawer into groups or categories?

Do you need little trays or baskets to divide those different groups?

Is this the best purpose for this drawer?

Is this the best place for the items in the drawer?

If the drawer wasn't there, where would those items land or live?

31 Days to an Organized Life

# NOTES                               Done ☐

_____

_____

_____

_____

## Tasks to Complete

☐ _____

☐ _____

☐ _____

☐ _____

## Other Projects Sparked by this Task

_____

_____

_____

Today I am celebrating my accomplishment by:

_____

Brenda Prinzavalli

# Organize Your Nightstand

What's the last thing you see before you go to sleep?
What's the first thing you see when you wake up?

There is a correlation between what we see and the message that gets planted in our mind.

Does that message send you off to slumberland with positive thoughts, ready to dream about your goals and joys?

When you wake up, does that message start your day with empowerment, joy and the confidence you need to take on a challenging day?

Create this space to be not only functional, but one that gives you a positive message.   Remove the clutter and tidy up when you make your bed each morning.
Also, make sure that if you wake up in the middle of the night, you can easily reach any needed items.

I also find it interesting that many times when someone is being interviewed or profiled, they ask, "What's on your nightstand right now?"  They are generally referring to what reading material, but since it's a popular question, there tends to be some meaning in what IS on your nightstand.

## NOTES

Done ☐

_____

_____

_____

_____

## Tasks to Complete

☐ _____

☐ _____

☐ _____

☐ _____

## Other Projects Sparked by this Task

_____

_____

_____

Today I am celebrating my accomplishment by:

_____

"My life is organized and simplified!"

# Organize the Bathroom Counter

Your bathroom counter should be 90% clear! Keep basic items like hand soap, a ring holder, and a small decorative item or two on the counter.

The goal is to have the counter space clear so when you pull out products for a specific task, there is room to set the products. The second part is to make it easy to put those products away. This makes daily items easy to use without the clutter for the other 23 hours and 45 minutes of the day.

HAIR DRYING AND STYLING
Get a basket for brushes, combs, hair dryer and clips. Pull out the basket, put it on the counter, dry and style your hair, then put the basket away.

MAKE-UP
Put make-up in a plastic drawer from a 3-4 tier drawer organizer that you can place under the sink. Then pull out the drawer, set it on the counter, do your make-up, then put the drawer away.

SHAVING
Depending on whether you use a wet razor or electric razor impacts how you store and use these tools. If you have an electric razor that has to be charged, can you hide a cord that runs into a cabinet space or only put the unit on the counter when you have to charge it once or twice a week. If you use a wet razor, get a container tall enough to hold shaving gel, razor and post shaving lotion in a vertical position.

## Organize the Bathroom Counter (cont.)

An important aspect of having a clutter-free and organized bathroom counter is that you spend less time doing the daily routines. You get out what you need, use it and put it away. No hunting and searching through the mass of products that live on the counter. You also don't have to shift things around on the counter to make space for the items for the next task.

The other bonus is for cleaning time; you don't have 14 splattered bottles to move before you wipe down the counter. AND you don't have 14 bottles that look horrible because they've been splattered and splashed upon.

One more bonus for those that use heating elements on your hair, fewer melted bottle edges from a curling iron!

## NOTES

Done ☐

_____

_____

_____

_____

## Tasks to Complete

☐ _____

☐ _____

☐ _____

☐ _____

## Other Projects Sparked by this Task

_____

_____

_____

Today I am celebrating my accomplishment by:

_____

## Other little personal actions

*Get up when the alarm goes off. You set it at that time when you planned your morning the night before, so stick with it.*

*Have good posture. It makes you feel in control and powerful and focused.*

Group Done ☐

# Personal

- Organize Someone Else Today

- What have you done for yourself lately?

- Wild Card Day

- Think Organized

- Goals

Brenda Prinzavalli

# Organize Someone Else Today

Today is a little different. I invite you into my joy for a day.

Today's task is not about your unfiled papers, the dishes in the sink or the project that waits for you to take action. Today is about someone else.

Find someone around you and create a little more organization in their life. You can tell them or make it a surprise. Better yet, you could **do A Random Act of Organizing**. **ARAO** we'll call it. It can be of any size and remember; sometimes the smallest changes can make the biggest difference.

A few very basic rules:

- Whatever you organize, it must be OK for you to see and move those items
- If the items are critical for health, finances, etc, they must be able to find the items easily

Now don't get me wrong, I know how many things you already do for those in your life, sometimes noticed, sometimes not. However, creating organization for someone else enhances your own organizational skills and discipline. It lets you experience a process from someone else's perspective that might shed light on how you look at organization.

## NOTES

Done ☐

_____

_____

_____

_____

## Tasks to Complete

☐ _____

☐ _____

☐ _____

☐ _____

## Other Projects Sparked by this Task

_____

_____

_____

Today I am celebrating my accomplishment by:

_____

# What have you done for yourself lately?

Many times when you think of organizing aspects of your day, it all focuses on tasks, jobs, errands, obligations and To Do lists. One aspect of life that deserves as much organizing as everything else is the time you organize for yourself. So, today review and organize the time and activities you have scheduled (or need to schedule) for yourself this week.

In case you don't have anything planned, here are some ideas; big and small!

- 5 minutes of meditation/prayer/quiet
- schedule a lunch with a friend
- get a personal treatment such as a manicure, massage or facial
- go for a bike ride - powered or pedal powered
- read a magazine or book
- exercise in whatever form is best for you
- work on a craft or building project that you enjoy
- Etc, etc, etc

31 Days to an Organized Life

# NOTES
Done ☐

_____

_____

_____

_____

## Tasks to Complete

☐ _____

☐ _____

☐ _____

☐ _____

## Other Projects Sparked by this Task

_____

_____

_____

Today I am celebrating my accomplishment by:

_____

# Wild Card Day

It's Wild Card Day! You get to pick how you spend the day related to organizing tasks!

- Catch Up
- Finish Up
- Rest Up
- Another Project on Your Mind

What is the best is for you to spend a Wild Card Day?

**Catch Up** ….. on Life

There is a good chance you have been going strong; staying focused on completing one task every day. The targeted focus of your time might have some other aspect of life that needs a catch up. You're in luck, catching up on any task certainly counts as organizing!

**Finish Up**… a Project

Go back to do one of the earlier days to finish a task.

**Rest Up**

Take a Break. Studies show that taking a break causes you to be more effective when you return to a task.

**Another Project** on Your Mind

One of the projects might have sparked an idea of something you need to organize so go for it!

It's all up to you to decide what the best is for you!

## NOTES

Done ☐

_____

_____

_____

_____

### Tasks to Complete

☐ _____

☐ _____

☐ _____

☐ _____

### Other Projects Sparked by this Task

_____

_____

_____

Today I am celebrating my accomplishment by:

_____

# Think Organized

If you choose to accept it, your mission for the day is to THINK organized. Before you plant a negative thought in your head, you must know that it is NOT "Mission Impossible" to change your thoughts and begin to experience how they impact your actions and results.

All day, know that you can make choices that support a more organized life. When you have a mindset that you will take more organized actions, guess what? You WILL take more organized actions and it will not only change slices of time throughout the day; it will change the outcome at the end of your day.

Create a reminder to help you keep organization at the forefront of your thoughts as it will be needed over and over. Here are a few possible times you might have the opportunity to make an organized choice:

Do I throw the coat on the couch or do I hang it up?

Do I call them back now or put it on my To Do list?

Should I sort the mail or put it on the corner of the desk?

I have 5 min, should I leave now or wait and hope traffic is OK?

......... and, if you listen and pay attention, all day you will hear the choices.

Will your mission for the day be possible?
I invite you to say YES and believe it!

Disclaimer: If you said YES, your computer will not self destruct in 30 seconds!

31 Days to an Organized Life

## NOTES         Done ☐

_____

_____

_____

_____

## Tasks to Complete

☐ _____

☐ _____

☐ _____

☐ _____

## Other Projects Sparked by this Task

_____

_____

_____

Today I am celebrating my accomplishment by:

_____

# Goals

Do you have goals for the next 90 days? Did you know that developing a plan and creating an organized structure for those goals are as important as the goals themselves? Otherwise those goals are just words.

Many people set their goals, start off strong by taking action, yet after a period of time, they fizzle out and the goals drift away. How can you stop that from happening? Whether a goal is to lose 10 lbs. or create a million dollars, if you have organization and a system in place to support your daily actions, you stand a much better chance of achieving the goals.

After you proclaim your goals, use the suggestions below to set up a plan and a system that will support you.

Organize Your Plan

1) Set your completion date and create a timeline.
2) Make a calendar for the duration of your goal that you can post or see on a daily basis.
3) Create a chart that shows the movement you are making toward the goal.
4) If you have a goal that requires specific steps, there might be an outline available that will give you the designated order of the steps.

Create a Support System
1) Set a specific time each day to review your actions and progress.
2) Tell someone your goal and how he or she can support you.
3) Get a coach.
4) Create a reward for achieving your goal.

So, what is the *other* most important component of working to accomplish your goals? Simply your intention! Good luck setting and reaching your dreams!

## NOTES

Done ☐

_____

_____

_____

_____

## Tasks to Complete

☐ _____

☐ _____

☐ _____

☐ _____

## Other Projects Sparked by this Task

_____

_____

_____

Today I am celebrating my accomplishment by:

_____

## Other little time actions

*Have a morning family conference to make sure everyone is set for the day and knows the schedule, appointments, dinnertime and events.*

*Fill up the car with gas before the week starts.*

Group Done ☐

# Schedule/Time

- Greetings for the Month

- Plan Your Week

- Errands Under Control

- Read for 15 Minutes

- PSPP Your Meals

Brenda Prinzavalli

# Greetings for the Month

This will save you time, gas and stress in the coming month.

The task is to prepare all greetings, gifts and remembrances that you want to acknowledge for one entire month.
- Make a list of all the birthdays, anniversaries, special occasions, or remembrances for the next month.
- Get the cards, gifts, make a dinner reservation, schedule a coffee date, etc for all those occasions!

You have several choices for cards:
- traditional greeting cards
- homemade cards
- e-cards

Decide which one suits your personality, your budget, your available time and your recipient.

- For traditional cards, buy them all now, address them, write them, stamp them and then put a sticky note on the card showing the day it should be mailed, taken to work, given to a neighbor or put on the mantel for someone in your household.
- For homemade cards, you only have to get out your supplies one time for making all the cards for one month. Address them, stamp them and note what day you should mail them.
- For e-cards, you maximize your search time because each card you read and review has the possibility of being the right card for someone on your list. Then you can schedule the card for delivery on a specific date. There's one more bonus with e-cards: When it actually gets delivered to the recipient, YOU can set the program to send you an email notice that it has been delivered. A great reminder to call them or acknowledge it's their special day.

While you are completing this task, there may be gifts and extra things you do to celebrate someone else. Get them purchased, wrapped, scheduled, ordered, etc.

## NOTES

Done ☐

_____

_____

_____

_____

### Tasks to Complete

☐ _____

☐ _____

☐ _____

☐ _____

### Other Projects Sparked by this Task

_____

_____

_____

Today I am celebrating my accomplishment by:

_____

# Plan Your Week

The one is best to complete on a Sunday or Monday.

It's the start of a full week and you have the opportunity to start it off right! Many times the "first" of something can set precedence, set a standard and set up for success. That's what you have an opportunity to do today.

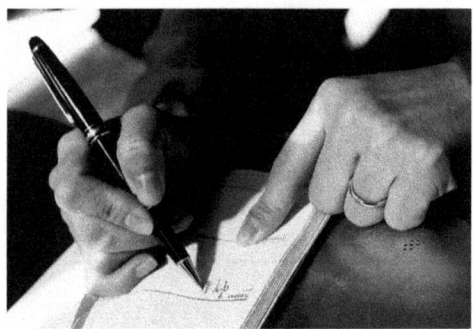

Today's task is to review and organize your week. You have many areas to consider that make demands of your time: work, family, exercise, appointments, tasks, social time, home maintenance, and sleep!

Depending on how scheduled you already have your week, this might simply be a review and confirmation that you have set your week up in the best way to get the best results.

When you plan your week, it supports your goals of achieving tasks and actions that are important to unfold as you desire.

Now, we know that unexpected things might pop up whether they are a challenge or for fun. However, the more you have crafted your precious time this week to support what you want to make happen in your life, the better chance you have for that to happen.

31 Days to an Organized Life

# NOTES

Done ☐

_____

_____

_____

_____

## Tasks to Complete

☐ _____

☐ _____

☐ _____

☐ _____

## Other Projects Sparked by this Task

_____

_____

_____

Today I am celebrating my accomplishment by:

_____

*"I put things away when I am finished using them!"*

# Errands Under Control

There are always things to return, exchange or pickup on a regular basis. Being disorganized about errands causes them to consume more of your time and energy. Take 15 minutes and make a plan for your errands for this week.

A great place to start is to ask several questions such as the ones listed below. Just adding one extra layer of organization helps you be more efficient and effective!

After you use these questions a couple of times in your planning stage, you'll start to automatically ask yourself these questions and organization of your errand time will continue to get easier and more efficient!

What is it that you have to do?

- return an item to a store
- pick up dry cleaning or alterations
- exchange an item

How will you keep track of these tasks & the items?

- make one short list for this week
- group them by type of task
- put tasks with a reminder in an electronic calendar
- write it on a whiteboard where you can see it

Errands Under Control (cont.)

Where are the items?

Find a location to put the items that will help you remember the item and the action. One idea is to place a basket by the door or in the car. Or put them in a bag with the receipt hanging on the door knob.

Where do you have to go to complete them?

Will you be driving by one of the locations at some point during the week? Plan to stop in while close by.

Who should complete the errand?

Who might be the closest to the location?

Who has the time?

Who has to be with to complete the action?

When is the best time to get them done?

Complete one task per day

Do them all in one day, evening or outing

Consider traffic conditions at time of errands

31 Days to an Organized Life

# NOTES          Done ☐

_____

_____

_____

## Tasks to Complete

☐ _____

☐ _____

☐ _____

☐ _____

## Other Projects Sparked by this Task

_____

_____

_____

Today I am celebrating my accomplishment by:

_____

Brenda Prinzavalli

# Read for 15 Minutes

As humans, by nature, we love to learn.  We strive to add new information to our knowledge base and expand our horizons.   To feed that urge, we harbor away books, articles, magazines, saved web pages and handouts that we want to read.....someday.

Today is the day!  Read that piece of information or story you saved!

The accumulation of things to read at a later date can become an organizing task in itself.  Unfortunately, you can spend more time shuffling and moving those items around than actually reading them.  Here are a couple of ideas and aspects to keep in mind about the items you saved to read at a future date.

Suggestions:

- Organize your day or week to include reading, learning or research time.
- Create a holding place for specific articles if they relate to an activity, hobby, travel destination or personal interest.
- Encourage those in your household to have a reading break.
- If you save articles from magazines, put a sticky note on that page or tear it out.  Then keep it with you so you can read when you are waiting for an appointment, a friend to meet you, on break at work or just when you find you have a moment available.

# NOTES

Done ☐

_____

_____

_____

_____

## Tasks to Complete

☐ _____

☐ _____

☐ _____

☐ _____

## Other Projects Sparked by this Task

_____

_____

_____

Today I am celebrating my accomplishment by:

_____

"I keep my life in balance by keeping it simple."

# PSPP Your Meals

The one is best to complete on a Saturday and/or Sunday.

This task will create many positive results for you in a variety of areas; budget, time, health, weight management, space and stress! With all those bonuses let's get started!

### PSPP Your Meals!

Plan, Shop, Prep and Portion your meals for the week.

Review each step in the process listed below. The goal is to wake up Monday morning and not have to plan or think about food for the week. The only thing you have to do all week is final touches on a meal and to enjoy the healthy, scrumptious and easy meals you prepared!

### Step 1 - Plan

Review the coming week

Look at what is going on this week and plan accordingly for quick meals, take away meals and mostly healthy choices.

**Try something new!**
If you save recipes and always want to try a new one, this is your chance to try one out for the week. Even trying one new recipe a week can add a fresh and new feeling to your meals.

**Plan** recipes and meals that use items in your pantry.
Using what you have will save on the grocery bill.

# PSPP Your Meals (cont.)

**Plan** recipes/meals that use similar special ingredients.
For example, if you need fresh cilantro for a meal, make sure you plan a meal or two that can use cilantro. While it's not the most expensive thing you have to purchase, cutting down on the food you waste will help with your budget.

**Make** a grocery list
Having a full list of needed groceries for the week based on your plan can save you time and money.

**Coupons**
Review coupons you have for items and advertised specials at stores. Star items on your grocery list that have coupons.

### Step 2 – Shop
If you have the option, pick a time to go grocery shopping when the grocery stores are less crowded and traffic is at a minimum, it will make your time go faster.

Do you need to visit multiple stores?

If you're like us, we shop at a couple of different stores based on where we can find good organic produce, products that match our ingredient criteria and also have the best price. So, plan to stop at the store where you buy your frozen or most perishable items last.

Green?
Take your reusable grocery bags!

Coupon Clipper?
Remember coupons and advertised specials!

## PSPP Your Meals (cont.)

### **Step 3 - Prep**

Prep Foods that need washing.

Most foods will last longer if they've been washed, especially in a veggie or fruit wash. It also cuts down the time needed when you go to eat it or when you use part for a recipe. Some items won't do well washed ahead of time like mushrooms, so you make the call whether to wash or not.

**Prep for recipes**
Whether it's portioning out ingredients, washing and chopping or getting out appliances needed for prep or cooking, doing it all at once can save time.

**Cook, Bake or Steam**
I'm all for eating the freshest food possible, but if the choice is to eat a good healthy portion of something made 3 days ago with great ingredients or doing a drive through, guess which one wins?

**Make Several** Dishes at One Time
Also, if you are in the kitchen preparing one dish, might as well do a few others at the same time. Use those minutes when you're waiting for something to boil, bake or rest by working on another recipe.

## PSPP Your Meals (cont.)

### **Step 4 - Portion**

Put in portion size containers for the week
If you take your lunch or would only have a single serving at one time (meaning don't make this for a family meal) put a serving in a storage container. It will help you when you are pulling items for your lunch, but it will also help you manage your portion sizes.

### **Freeze**
If it is something that will freeze well and it makes an extra large batch or it is easy to do a double batch, freeze in portion or family meal size containers. This makes it easy on a busy day to take a prepared dish out of the freezer in the morning, let it thaw during the day and you're ready in the evening with a healthy dish. It is also something that stretches the return on investment of prep time for dishes that freeze because you can make double or triple dishes at one time.

### **Cheat Sheet**
For the items that you have partially prepped, create a little cheat sheet that gives you the final touches you need to complete before serving. Either jot it down and put it on the container or if it is more detailed, leave the recipe out or put a sticky note on the page in a cookbook for quick reference.

31 Days to an Organized Life

# NOTES

Done ☐

_____

_____

_____

_____

## Tasks to Complete

☐ _____

☐ _____

☐ _____

☐ _____

## Other Projects Sparked by this Task

_____

_____

_____

Today I am celebrating my accomplishment by:

_____

# Congratulations!

You took action this month to regain your sanity and take control of your life this month by organizing critical areas of your life. You should be oozing with pride and satisfaction! You might have learned a little bit about yourself along the way.

## What I learned about myself

_____

_____

_____

_____

The next important step in this process is to make sure that the spaces and actions you organized STAY organized. For each mini-project you completed, consider what daily action or habit do you need to practice to keep your organization sustained. Also, plan how often you need to take action to refresh and maintain a space or process.

# Other Projects Sparked this Month

_____

_____

_____

_____

_____

_____

_____

## I am celebrating my month of accomplishments by:

_____

_____

## Checklist

To support your tracking of each project outside of this book, you can download a one sheet checklist to assist you with marking off the mini-projects you have completed.

To access the download link for the checklist, follow one of the following paths:

Type in this Tiny URL that will take you to our website page and then follow the download process.
http://tinyurl.com/bw5wkob

Type in this Full URL that will take you to our website page and then follow the download process.
http://www.brendaprinzavalli.com/products/organizing-book/31daycklistform/

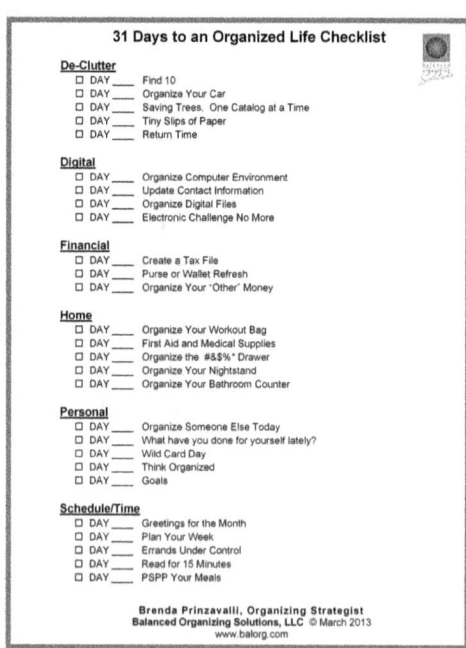

# Organizing Resources

### Consulting Services
that create organization
in Professional and Personal Life
*Balanced Organizing Solutions, LLC*
www.brendaprinzavalli.com


### Organized Home Based Business
Strategy for organizing a Direct Selling
or Network Marketing Business.
Simple, easy, geared toward getting results
www.organizedhbb.com


### The Accomplishment Journal Series
A **proven system** that helps you get more out
of your day and your business, spend more time
with your family and do what *you* want to do.
www.accomplishmentjournal.com


### Marketing Organized
*Marketing Organized* delivers a step-by-step guide
for creating results with proven marketing strategies.
A unique pairing of a marketing expert
with an organizing expert.
**New Audio and Workbook Set Available!**
www.marketingorganized.com


### Newsletters
Want to receive GREAT tips on organizing?
Sign up for the Organizing eNews at
http://www.brendaprinzavalli.com/newsletter/


Brenda Prinzavalli, Organizing Strategist
brenda@balorg.com
702-375-0585

## About the Author

Brenda Prinzavalli shares her passion for life through sharing her passion for applying organizational philosophies to all areas of your personal and professional life.

Even thought her ability to communicate organizing strategies has been with her from the start, in 2003 she made it her life's mission.

Brenda founded **Balanced Organizing Solutions, LLC**, a professional organizing service, to assist businesses and individuals in finding solutions for their busy lives. She offers on-site and virtual consulting, as well as hands-on organizing services. She delivers upbeat and interactive training programs, corporate workshops and seminars that encourage audiences to transform their lives through mastery of behaviors that lead to control of their actions and environment.

She holds a master of elementary education from the University of Nevada, Las Vegas, and a bachelor of elementary education from the University of Iowa. She and her husband, Brian, currently reside in Las Vegas, Nevada.

Additional information available on the following websites:

Balanced Organizing Solutions, LLC  www.brendaprinzavalli.com

In the Media links  http://www.brendaprinzavalli.com/media/news/

FOX 5 Las Vegas MORE! Dream Team Organization Editor
http://www.fox5vegas.com/morevegas/index.html

Co-Author and Co-Developer
The Accomplishment Journal Series
www.accomplishmentjournal.com

Co-Author and Co-Developer
Marketing Organized
http://www.marketingorganized.com

"I love being organized!"

www.ingramcontent.com/pod-product-compliance
Lightning Source LLC
Chambersburg PA
CBHW071734040426
42446CB00012B/2352